penguins

A PHOTOGRAPHIC CELEBRATION

2007 Metro Books

ISBN-13: 978-0-7607-9028-1
ISBN-10: 0-7607-9028-0

Printed and bound in Singapore

1 3 5 7 9 10 8 6 4 2

penguins

A PHOTOGRAPHIC CELEBRATION

edited by lisa purcell

METRO BOOKS
NEW YORK

"It's practically impossible to look at a penguin and feel angry."
—JOE MOORE

All penguins, living and extinct, fall into the order Spheniciformes
and the family Spheniscidae. There are six genera and between 16 and 19 recognized species.

The *Spheniscus*, or banded penguins, so named for the black stripes that cross their breasts, are the Humboldt, Magellanic, African, and Galápagos penguins. They live in the warmest climates penguins can tolerate in South Africa and South America.

Crested, or *Eudyptes*, penguins—the Macaroni, Rockhopper, Fiordland, Erect-crested, and Snares—are easily identified by their bright yellow or orange crests. They all live on the subantarctic islands of New Zealand and South America.

Collectively known as the "brush-tailed penguins,"
Chinstraps, Gentoos, and Adélies are members of the *Pygoscelis* species.
They breed on the Antarctic continent and surrounding islands.

Megadyptes antipodes, or the Yellow-eyed penguin, has a genus to itself.
These denizens of the coastal areas of southern New Zealand
and neighboring subantarctic islands display a swath of yellow feathers
that starts at the chin and extends up the head.
As their name suggests, their eyes are also yellow.

Penguin royalty? The *Aptenodytes* penguins—Emperors and Kings—are also called "the great penguins" because of their impressive size. Both species live in Antarctica, and Kings also live on the subantarctic islands, Tierra del Fuego, and the Falklands.

A tiny penguin with a lot of names, *Eudyptula minor* is known
as the Little Blue or Fairy penguin—or just plain Little or Blue.
The New Zealand Māori also call them Kororā.
They breed around the entire coastline of New Zealand
as well as southern Australia and Tasmania.

Penguin species are found on every
continent in the southern hemisphere.

The first written documentation of a penguin sighting was in 1497. A sailor rounding Cape Horn with explorer Vasco da Gama described them as "large as ganders and with a cry resembling the cry of asses."

The ancestors of today's penguins stopped flying approximately 60 million years ago.

Most penguins are excellent divers.

Penguins are highly social birds, usually living in colonies,
and swimming and feeding in groups.

During the breeding season, many penguin species come ashore to nest in huge colonies. These colonies, called "rookeries," can consist of hundreds of thousands of penguins.

In general, penguins are dimorphic; you cannot tell apart the males from the females.

Although males and females look alike, males usually have larger bodies and bills.

The penguin family name of Spheniscidae comes the Greek word for wedge, referring to the penguin's curved flipper-wings.

Where did the name "penguin" come from?
Some say it was first used by Spanish sailors in reference
to the amount of fat on these birds' bodies (*penguigo*).
Others say it comes from the Welsh term
pen gwyn, which means "white head."

The Chinstrap penguin was named for the black band that frames its face.

"[T]he one thing upon which we should all agree is that it is enough that penguins are beautiful birds."
—Lloyd Spencer Davis

A group of penguin chicks is called a "crèche."

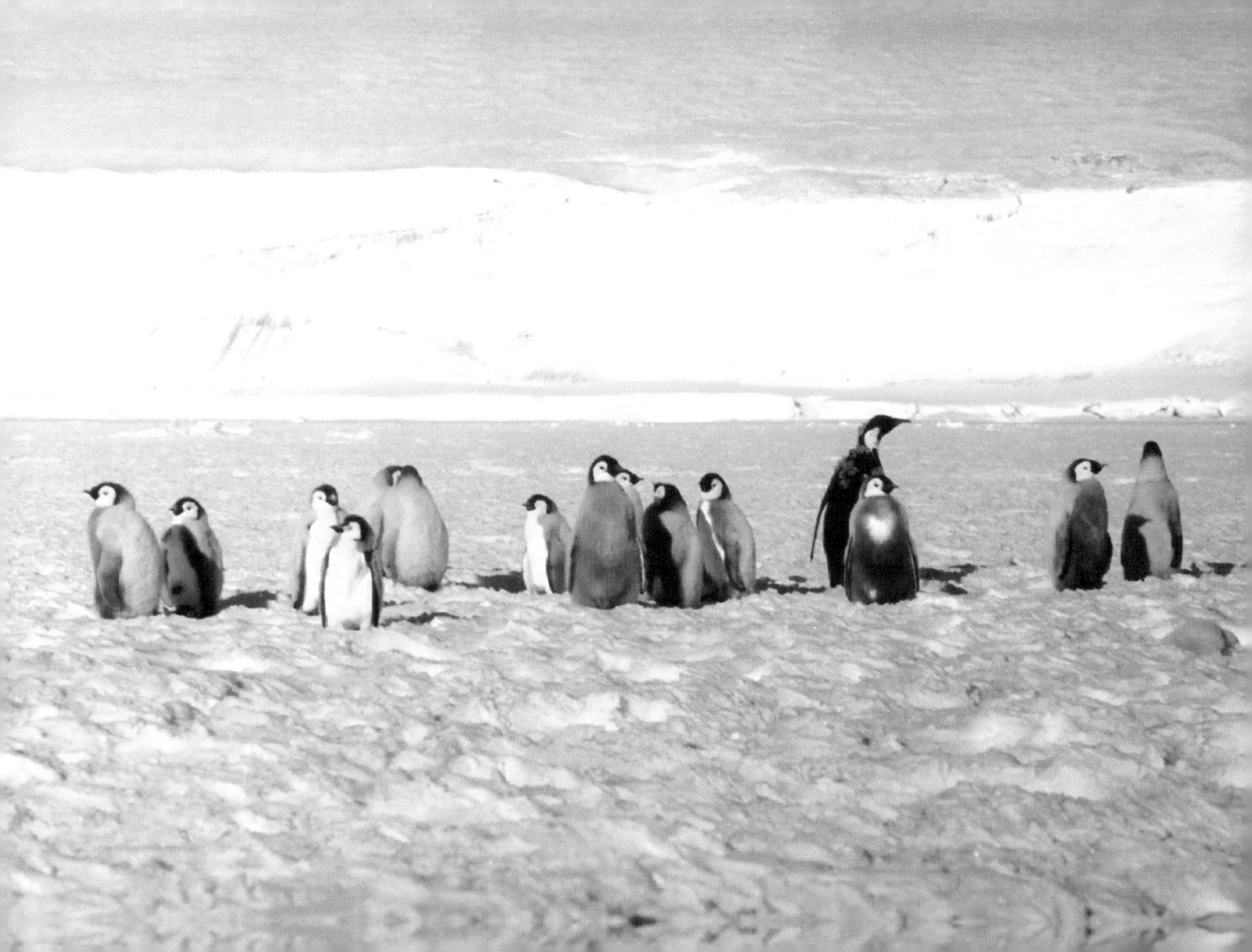

A penguin's feet looks like they are covered
with reptilian skin, with scales varying in color.

Penguins are countershaded; in other words,
their fronts and backs contrast with one another.
All of the species have white undersides
and dark—usually black—upper sides.

Although their species name is *patagonicas*, King penguins no longer breed in Patagonia. By the nineteenth century, seal hunters had wiped out all of their colonies there.

It is now illegal to hunt penguins throughout most of the southern hemisphere.

When overheated, penguins hold their flippers
away from their sides to cool down.

Penguins that live in warmer climates have featherless patches on their faces, which help to release heat.

Penguins have the most efficient, streamlined shape of any animal—or even any man-made design.

The bills of penguins vary in shape and size.
Some are hooked, which helps them grab onto prey.

An Antarctic water park?
Penguins seem to dive for the sheer fun of it,
plunging into the water from cliffs and ice shelves
and then hopping back out to do it all over again.
At times, long queues of penguins can be seen
at the water's edge, waiting to take their next turns.

The first generation of penguins, which are estimated to have surfaced approximately 60 million years ago, are called *Waimanu manneringi*. Scientists think they resembled today's Yellow-eyed penguin.

How do Galápagos penguins survive so close to the equator?
The Cromwell Current brings icy waters north up the South American coast.

Studies have shown that most penguins return to the same nesting sites year after year.

Penguin chicks can take up to three days to make their way out of their shells.

The first penguin fossil was discovered in 1848.
The actual bird probably lived between
23 and 34 million years ago.

One motivation behind the switch from flying bird to a flightless one
may have been the abundance of food that the ocean holds beneath its surface.

Because they only thrive in the truly frigid Antarctic climate, Adélie and Emperor penguins are rarely held in captivity.

In honor of their harsh, piercing voices, Chinstrap penguins are also called "Stonecrackers."

In a technique known as "tobogganing,"
penguins travel by sliding on their bellies through the snow.

Before their annual period of fasting—usually around
the breeding season—penguins build a fat layer
that will provide them with energy during the fast.

Penguins are some of the most adaptive species of animals. They breed in climates with average temperatures as cold as minus 75 to as hot as 104 degrees Fahrenheit.

Some penguins spend six months at a time in the ocean before coming ashore.

Banding together helps deter predators.
A predator is more likely to attack a
solitary penguin than venture into a colony of birds.

Because penguins are warm-blooded, they can convert food into energy quickly.

A penguin's black-and-white coloring is effective camouflage.
To a potential predator swimming below, its white belly looks like the sky,
while its black back blends in with the water to protect it from predators above.

Rockhoppers are surely some of the most colorful of the penguins,
with a yellow stripe above each eye that projects out into a shock of yellow feathers,
bright red eyes, a reddish bill to match, and pink legs and feet.

Humboldt fledglings look like drab versions of their parents,
and lack the distinctive stripes that will later identify them as banded penguins.

What were once the wings of its flying ancestor
are now narrow flippers that help a penguin swim.

Penguins usually swallow their food whole.

Commercial fishing has devastated Rockhoppers breeding on the Falkland Islands. From an estimated 2.5 million pairs in 1984, numbers plummeted to a mere 300,000 by the mid-1990s.

The average body temperature of penguins ranges between 100 and 102 degrees Fahrenheit.

Penguins often sleep side by side and usually with their bills tucked behind a flipper.

Young penguins may migrate hundreds of miles
from their place of birth, but most tend to return
to their original rookeries to molt and breed.

The Little Blue penguin is able to breed year-round and has the shortest breeding cycle among penguins.

Penguins take, on average, between three and eight years to mature into adulthood.

"Ecotourism" has become increasingly popular,
with cruise ships touring the subantarctic waters
in sight of penguin colonies. Tourists, however, should
be careful to avoid interfering with the birds' normal activities.

Penguins tend to live on lands free of ground predators. With their inability to fly, they would be easy prey.

Scientists think that millions of penguins visit the uninhabited Zavodovski Island in the South Sandwich Islands each spring to nest.

A community of 5 million Adélie penguins can consume up to 18 million pounds of krill and other small fish a day.

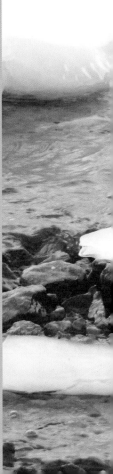

Adélie and Gentoo penguins have been known
to reduce their heart rates from about 100 beats per minute
to about 20 beats per minute when diving.

Although it is usually difficult to distinguish
between the sexes, during the breeding season
it can be a bit easier to spot a female penguin:
when mating, males may leave
muddy footprints on their mates' backs.

Some male King penguins fast for up to 50 days
during courtship and the first incubation shift.

Magellanic penguins are named after Portuguese explorer Ferdinand Magellan, who first spotted them during his 1519 voyage around the tip of South America.

The Little Blue penguin fits its name—
at only 16 inches high and about 2.2 pounds,
it is the smallest of the penguin species.

Their dark feathers help to absorb heat
from the sun, keeping penguins warm in colder climates.

For brief moments, it appears as if penguins can fly. When traveling at high speeds, they often dive in and out of water. This is called "porpoising."

Why to penguins waddle?
Their short stubby legs make it difficult for them to walk.

Although some prehistoric penguins were as tall as humans, the largest living penguin, the Emperor, stands on average about three and a half feet tall and weighs a hefty 75 pounds.

Want to see a penguin in the wild?
Boulders Beach in South Africa is the best place
to observe colonies of African penguins.

"I have often had the impression that, to penguins,
man is just another penguin—different, less predictable, occasionally violent,
but tolerable company when he sits still and minds his own business."
—BERNARD STONEHOUSE

Most birds shed a few feathers at a time in the spring.
Penguins molt their entire coat of feathers at once.

Penguins sometimes build nests made of pebbles and grass.

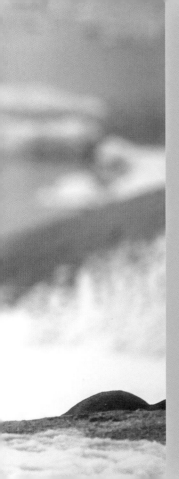

Penguin sing-a-longs?
When one penguin calls,
it often inspires its neighbors to join in.

One of the most common reasons behind an unsuccessful breeding is the mistiming between hopeful parents. When a male is left too long without food, he will sometimes leave the eggs before the female comes back to the nest for her turn to incubate them.

Penguins that reside in colder climates have longer feathers than their warm-weather cousins.

At their breeding colonies, King penguins are highly gregarious. Despite the density of these colonies, fighting among birds is rare.

Emperor chicks are almost always only children.

Despite their limited range—the Falkland Islands and parts of South America—populations of Magellanic penguins remain high, with at least 1.8 million known breeding pairs.

The average lifespan of penguins ranges between 15 and 20 years.

A penguin can control its body temperature
by either facing toward or away from the sun.

Some penguins spend almost three-quarters of their lives at sea.

Emperor penguins endure the coldest temperatures
of all animals during the frigid Antarctic winter.

Keeping cool is not always easy for the super-insulated penguins. When overheated, their flippers and feet may redden, and they will fluff their feathers, pant, and eat snow.

Southern hemisphere southpaws?
An MIT study revealed that 80 percent of penguins are lefties,
using their left flippers for everything from nest building
to shoving a neighbor out of the way.

Penguins use their webbed feet as rudders
to help them turn while swimming.

Although penguins can no longer fly in the air,
they "fly" underwater, reaching speeds of up to 10 miles per hour.

"... it will be a lonely knee-high black-and-white penguin waddling up the snow-covered beach that will steal your heart."
—LLOYD SPENCER DAVIS

The oldest-known African penguin in the wild was recorded at 24 years of age, but several aquarium-living individuals have lived to be 40.

Very similar to divers' wet suits, penguins' feathers
are specially designed for freezing waters.
They are small, stiff, interlocking, and almost
impossible to ruffle by wind or water.

To avoid the heat of their South American home,
Magellanic penguins dig burrows
that form huge underground "cities."

Penguins are often seen "body-surfing" through the waves onto land.

At approximately 70 per square inch, penguin feathers are the densest of any bird's.

While swimming, a penguin keeps its head tucked low between its shoulders and keeps its feet close to its body.

Although most penguins build a nest for their eggs,
Emperor and King penguins balance their eggs on top of their feet.

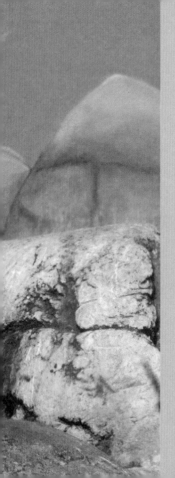

Where does the Rockhopper get its name?
To reach its nest on steep, rocky perches,
it holds its feet together and bounces from ledge to ledge.

An entire population of Humboldt penguins was displaced from its home in Peru when the thick layer of guano (otherwise known as bird poop), which it used as nesting grounds, was commercially mined for use as agricultural fertilizer.

Although krill is the main source of food for most penguins, squid is a popular alternative for some of them. King penguins have been known to eat six pounds of squid in one feeding.

Penguins are very good at estimating from a distance the height of shore, rocks, or ice. They can speed toward land and pop out of the water to heights of up to seven feet before making an upright landing.

Macaroni penguins keep it simple—they scrape a shallow hole in mud or gravel among rocks to form crude nests.

Believe it or not, National Penguin Egg Day was once a reality in the Falkland Islands. November 9 was set aside each year for the hunting of penguin eggs.
This tradition almost eradicated entire penguin colonies near Port Stanley.

Penguins are near-sighted when on land, but have excellent vision underwater.

When it comes to parenting, penguin parents split duties.
In some cases, mom will leave to gather food for their new arrivals.
In other cases, she will incubate the egg while dad guards her.

The simple black-and white coloring of Adélie penguins draws comparisons to chubby little men in feathery tuxedos.

Penguins spend a good amount of time each day preening their feathers.
Their feathers must be maintained and kept in top condition
to ensure that they remain waterproof and insulative.

Male Emperor penguins can fast for up to 120 days during courtship, breeding, and the entire incubation period.

In order to survive in the temperate zone,
African penguins tend to be active at their breeding sites
only at the cooler hours of dusk and dawn.
During the heat of the day, they head to sea for
a swim or loaf about the beach in groups.

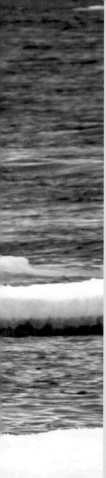

Penguin predators in the water include
leopard seals, fur seals, sea lions, sharks, and killer whales.

The Macaroni penguin may have gotten its name from the eighteenth-century slang term *macaroni*. Macaronis were flashily dressed young men, who wore bright feathers in their hats.

Penguins will grow their first full set of adult plumage by the age of one.

Little Blue penguins and most of the crested species like a good fight—regularly pitching bloody brawls during the breeding season.

"They are extraordinarily like children, these little people of the Antarctic world, either like children, or like old men, full of their own importance and late for dinner, in their black tail-coats and white shirt-fronts—and rather portly withal."
—APSLEY CHERRY-GARRARD

Penguins can be categorized into two feeding groups—inshore feeders and offshore feeders. Inshore feeders take short foraging trips, usually no more than 12 miles away from shore. Offshore feeders will journey hundreds of miles to locate food.

Land predators of penguin chicks and eggs include foxes, snakes, dogs, and cats.

At sea, penguins can recognize the calls of their colony mates.

Fidelity rates vary among penguin species and breeding locations.
Pairs that stay in the same area year-round may mate for life, but only
15 percent of those that must part get back together the next breeding season.

A common bonding ritual between penguins
is the offering of a stone from one to another.

Penguins are very competitive
when mating is involved. It is not abnormal
for a female to drive away the new lover of her old partner.

The "perfect" rock is a valuable commodity to Adélies and Chinstraps, which use them to construct their nests. It is not unusual for penguins to brangle over stones—and even steal them from unwary neighbors.

Although most penguins can stay underwater for about a minute only,
Gentoo and Adélie penguins have set records of up to seven minutes below the surface.

Contrary to popular belief,
penguins and polar bears are never neighbors.
They live in opposite hemispheres.

Residents of Cape Town, South Africa,
treasure their local penguins—and have been key to their survival.
When an oil spill covered nearly all of the penguins at Robben Island,
more than 12,000 Capetonians gathered for three months
to meticulously clean the oil-slicked birds.

A thick lining of fat helps to keep penguins warm.

Penguins start to breed between the ages of two and three years old.

When a male wants to attract a mate, he will arch his back, stretch out his neck, and let out a long, honking call.

To a human, it may seem that if you've heard one penguin you've heard them all. This, however, is not true. Each penguin's voice is as unique as a fingerprint.

Birds are measured from the tips of their feet
to the points of their beaks while lying down.

A chick has an "egg tooth" on the tip of its beak that helps it to break through the shell of its egg.

The penguin courtship period usually lasts from two to three weeks.

Gentoo penguins brighten up the basic black-and-white penguin suit with white "bonnets" and striking red-orange beaks and feet.

Immature penguins lack the distinct markings of adults,
and are often muted shades of brownish gray rather than glossy black.

African penguins are monogamous, and
pairs generally return to the same colony—
and even the same nesting site—year after year.

Galápagos penguins are the rarest of the penguin species,
with fewer than a thousand breeding pairs on the western
Galápagos islands of Fernandina, Isabela, and, possibly, Bartolomé.

Sure, they look cute to us, but Chinstraps are the most combative of the penguin species. It's not unusual for these bold penguins to pick raucous fights with one another.

Black feathers cover most of the beak on the Adélie penguin.

Penguins produce a special oil from a gland at the base of their tails. They often spread this fine oil all over their bodies to help keep their feathers watertight.

Kings are the second-largest penguin; only Emperors are larger.

How do you tell the King apart from the Emperor penguin?
The teardrop-shaped ear patch is closed and a bright orange on the King;
the Emperor ear patch is open and a subtler yellow.

A Little Blue penguin has anywhere between 300 to 400 percent more feathers than a flying bird of equal size.

When penguins are close to shore they often lift their heads out of the water as if to assess how close they are to land.

King chicks wear fuzzy brown feather "coats."
They look so different from their parents
that early explorers thought the brown chicks
were an entirely separate species—
which they called the "woolly penguin."

How do you tell one banded penguin species from the others?
The largest of them, the Magellanic, has two bands instead of the single band
of the others. A wide black stripe circles the chin and another is in the shape of
an upside down horseshoe on its stomach. Black spots are scattered across its chest.

Three subspecies of the Rockhopper penguin
can be found world-wide: the Southern, Eastern, and Northern.
All of them are among the smallest of the penguin species.

The longest penguin trip tracked
was 1,700 miles, made by an Adélie.

The Little Blue penguin lives a mostly nocturnal life to avoid predators such as gulls, peregrines, snakes, rats, and lizards.

Although most penguins seem to have internal global positioning systems, some penguins do get lost. Those that are found in unlikely spots are referred to as "vagrants."

Smaller penguins tend to live shorter lives. The longest-surviving Little Blue penguin in the wild was 17 years old.

The increase of daylight hours during early spring signals to penguins that breeding season has arrived.

King penguins were once hunted for their meat
and feathers, and boiled down for their oil.

Oil spills have proven one of the deadliest threats to penguins. Oil is not only poisonous when ingested, but it also clogs feathers, destroying their insulation.

For penguins, the "guard" stage consists of the first two or three weeks of life when they must be cared for 24 hours a day.

Although Emperors endure the harshest of climates,
they have the highest survival rate among penguins.

"Fledgling" is the term used to refer to immature penguins that are ready to strike out on their own.

Unique among penguins, Emperor dads produce and secrete a curdlike substance from their esophaguses. If a chick hatches before mom returns from her foraging at sea, he can feed this "penguin milk" to his chick, ensuring its survival for up to two weeks.

On average, a penguin will eat between 10 and 14 percent of its body weight in fish each day.

Penguins have three hooked toes on each foot. The hooks help them to grip ice and slippery rocks as they walk.

Adélies are the smallest of the penguins
living on the Antarctic continent.

Underwater landmarks may be as important
to penguins as aboveground ones. They have been known
to keep to the same route for years, passing by the same markers.

With a total breeding population of just a bit more than 300,000,
Gentoos are the least numerous of the penguins found on the subantarctic islands.

Chinstrap penguins tend to dive at noon or at midnight.

Penguins may use the sun as a compass.
It is normal for them to start migrations at sundown.

Male and female penguins usually approach
each other in bows as signs of peace.

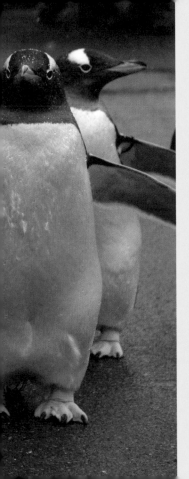

"If I could be a bird, I think I'd be a penguin, because then I could walk around on two feet with a lot of other guys like me."
—JACK HANDEY

The wear and tear of a penguin's day-to-day activities means that it must molt all of its feathers once a year.

Penguins usually sleep more during times of fasting to conserve energy.

Although penguins all look alike, a penguin parent can pick its child out of thousands of other birds.

Global warming will have a severe impact on the penguin population in the future. Penguins have already lost valuable habitats and are being forced to find new places to live.

Males are the first to arrive at rookeries.
Once there, they choose nesting sites, which they defend
until the females arrive and lay eggs.

Why do Gentoo penguins often successfully raise two chicks in a season? One reason is that Gentoo parents can stay close to their young when foraging because food is abundant near the shores where they nest.

As many as 500,000 penguins have been counted on 500 acres of land in Antarctica.

The feathers on a penguin's stomach
are usually the first to fall out during molt.

Carotenoid pigments are responsible for the orange-yellow feathers that are found on King and Emperor penguins.

Nest collapse and flooding are two major threats to
burrow-nesting penguins, such as Humboldts and Magellanics.

The nimble Chinstrap penguin can climb using all four limbs and jumps large distances to reach footholds in its rocky environment.

An Emperor penguin's nasal cavity is specially adapted to conserve heat that is normally lost during exhalation.

White-flippered penguins are usually considered a subspecies of the Little Blue, although some scientists classify them as a separate species.

It can take between 33 and 64 days of incubation before penguin eggs hatch. Smaller eggs tend to need shorter incubation periods.

Human presence has been known to raise the heart rates of penguins.

Lack of food during some winter months allows
starvation to claim the lives of up to half of King chicks.

Nils Olav, a King penguin, is the mascot
for the Royal Norwegian Guard.

"Penguins mate for life. That doesn't surprise me much because they all look alike. It's not like they're going to meet a really new, great-looking penguin someday."
—ANONYMOUS

Some penguins can sleep as they float at sea.

Even though a penguin stays at sea
for weeks at a time, its skin will stay dry.

Adélie penguins don't drink water, but instead eat snow.

When it reaches about a month old,
a Gentoo chick leaves the nest to go join other chicks
while it waits for mom or dad to bring it food.

A penguin may look fluffy and perfect for cuddling,
but their feathers are actually rough and prickly.

The Emperor penguin never walks on land that is not covered in ice.

Little Blue penguins have strange nesting habits.
They are known to clamber far up steep coasts to dig burrows
in the soil, or they select very particular spots within sea caves.

King penguins prefer breeding sites on flat coastal plains close to sandy beaches.

In preparation for its molting period,
a penguin may increase its body weight
by as much as 50 percent.

Chinstrap penguins have
had a 400-percent increase
in population over the last 25 years.

A chick vibrates its bill against its parent's to signal that it is hungry.

The dark coloring of a penguin's back is produced by the abundant amount of the pigment melanin in its feathers.

Because there are only three main calls used by penguins, body language can mean the difference between a peaceful and a violent meeting between two penguins.

Penguins engage in two types of dives: V dives and U dives.
V dives are usually shorter, with less time spent at the bottom.

Penguins are distant relatives of dinosaurs—as are all birds.

Should I stay or should I go?
Sometimes it seems as if a penguin just can't make up its mind
when standing at the water's edge. A little shove from
behind may be all it needs to take that first step . . .

"When you say the penguins are coming back,
I think that's wonderful because that shows that it's not just the penguins;
that shows that the whole food chain is being renewed,
that you're also increasing the marine habitat."
—SUSAN GEORGE

The large chicks of African penguins
that gather in crèches are sometimes called "wombles."

Little Blue penguins got their name from the bluish hue of their backs.

Humans would last only a few minutes in the Antarctic seas,
but penguins thrive in the icy waters.

Penguin feathers are symmetrical, short, and stiff,
unlike the feathers of most other birds,
which are asymmetrical, long, and flexible.

Penguins were once thought to be feathered fish.

Penguins are not the only animals with torpedo-shaped bodies.
This shape is common to other sea dwellers, such as sea lions and dolphins.

Kings have a long brooding period
(about a year), so unlike most penguins,
they raise only two chicks every three years.

Parent penguins feed chicks by regurgitating food into their mouths.

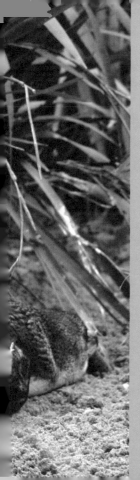

New Zealand is considered the world's penguin capital;
it is home to 9 out of 16 confirmed species.

The only part of a penguin that is not insulated is its feet.

Penguin feathers, like all other feathers, are thought to have evolved from scales.

There are an estimated one million breeding pairs of King penguins.

Of all seabirds, only the storm petrel lives
farther south than the Adélie penguin.

It is unclear how fledglings know exactly what to do and where to go for food, but adults do not help them find their way.

Gentoos are the speediest of the penguins—
in fact, they are the fastest underwater swimming birds,
reaching speeds of just over 22 miles per hour.

An equal number of male and female chicks are born
but by the time penguins mature into adulthood,
males will outnumber females.

Papua, the species name of the Gentoo,
refers to Papua, New Guinea—
although there are no penguins to be found there.

Penguins rarely feed chicks that do not belong to them.

Adélie penguins mate in the Antarctic summer, with its 24-hour daylight, and are therefore the most observed species during the breeding season.

To female penguins, large males are generally considered the most attractive.

Although penguins are known for epic migratory behaviors,
not all penguins migrate. Some stay in the same location year-round.

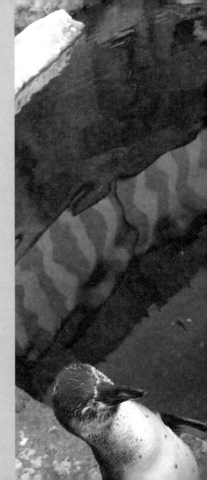

"It is not the strongest of the species that survives,
nor the most intelligent that survives.
It is the one that is the most adaptable to change."
—CHARLES DARWIN

The scientific name of the Rockhopper penguin,
Eudyptes chrysocome, translates as "golden-haired good diver."

A penguin keeps its eggs warm with a special brood patch
that is like a zippered opening leading to its warm skin.

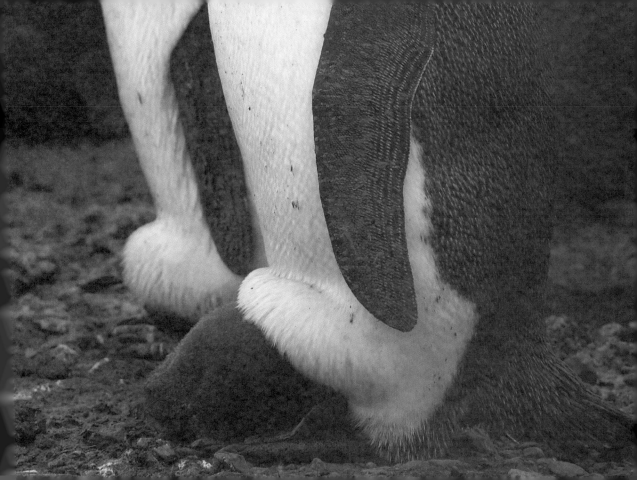

At present, zoos house thousands of penguins worldwide.

Aptenodytes, the genus name of King and Emperor penguins, means "flightless diver."

Known as leucistic or isabelline, there are rare "blond" individuals that lack the melanin that gives the black color to other penguins.

Penguins *do* have ears, and they're in the same place as a human's.
But unlike human ears, penguin ears are not external;
the ear openings are covered by feathers.

The species name of the Galápagos penguin, *mendiculus*, means "little beggar."

Although all birds are bipedal, penguins are the most upright, making them resemble humans when they walk.

"Because their legs are set so low down on their bodies, penguins stand upright and perhaps it is this similarity to ourselves that makes penguins so attractive to people."
—PAULINE REILLY

Pygoscelis, the genus name of Adélie, Gentoo, and Chinstrap penguins, means "rump legged."

Penguin nests are often nestled in caves and crevices.

When a penguin falls, it often uses its beak to flip itself over.
Once on its front, it is able to flip its feet forward and stand up.

Adélie penguins were named in the 1830s
by French explorer Durmont d'Urville, in honor of his wife, Adéle.

While molting, penguins are extremely vulnerable and are less capable of keeping themselves warm.

Emperor penguins hold the record for deepest dive at a depth of 1,755 feet.

Don't go near the water!
The downy feathers of penguin chicks
keep them warm, but they are not waterproof.

The "hand" bones of penguins are fused together. This helps them propel themselves through water.

Penguins do not have teeth.

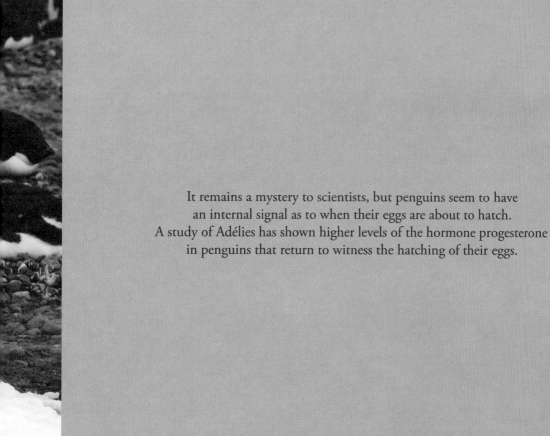

It remains a mystery to scientists, but penguins seem to have
an internal signal as to when their eggs are about to hatch.
A study of Adélies has shown higher levels of the hormone progesterone
in penguins that return to witness the hatching of their eggs.

Along with the animal predators
that Little Blue penguins face on land,
a new enemy has emerged—the car.

Penguins thrive in areas where most animals would not even survive. Emperor penguins breed in the heart of the subzero Antarctic winter.

"Take it all in all, I do not believe anybody on earth
has a worse time than an Emperor penguin."
—APSLEY CHERRY-GERRARD

King chicks are born naked and grow their down
over the course of their first few weeks of life.
This makes it imperative that their parents keep them warm.

A penguin's bill is as sharp as a knife. It is advised that humans stay clear to avoid a nasty cut.

Penguins maintain "penguin highways" from their nesting sites to the sea.

Penguins can use their beaks as weapons.

Most penguins lay one clutch of eggs per year.
African penguins can lay two clutches if the weather permits.

African penguins are also known as Blackfooted penguins.

The population of African penguins has decreased by 90 percent over the last 70 years. The drop can be attributed to increased fishing, egg hunting, and oil pollution.

Humboldt penguins are named after Alexander von Humboldt,
a Prussian naturalist and explorer of the nineteenth century,
who first described these birds to Western observers.

Chicks, like human babies, are fed small amounts of food every few hours during the early days of life.

Name that tune?
After the female King lays her egg,
she and her mate stay together, and each
of them sings a song to the other.
If they become separated, they
will know each other by these songs.

With its honking, braylike call, it's not surprising that
the African penguin was once known as the "Jackass" penguin.

A penguin has a spiny tongue to help it swallow slippery fish.

Yellow-eyed penguins are featured
on the New Zealand five-dollar bill.

Antarctic breeders usually build nests of stones to allow for drainage.

Although not usually visible, penguins have knees
just as humans do—only theirs are covered with feathers.

Penguins sleep in a variety of positions.
They can even sleep while standing.

What do you call a group of penguins on land?
There is no official name, but delegates
at the International Penguin Conference in 2000
agreed that it should be called a "waddle."

The International Penguin Conference delegates
also chose to call a group of penguins at sea a "raft."

With their large size and impressive endurance,
Emperors are thought to be the strongest of the penguin species.

Adélie chicks grow the fastest of all penguins.

The scientific name of the Little Blue penguin,
Eudyptula minor, means "good little diver."

Penguin mates have several ways to greet each other.
One way is to face each other, bow, and then
point their bills skyward and trumpet together.

A penguin's short legs and wedge-shaped tail is thought to aid it in standing for long periods of time without getting tired.

In order to protect themselves from the harsh winds of the Antarctic winter, male Emperor penguins huddle together in groups of up to 5,000 while incubating their eggs. These groups shift ever so slowly—earning them the name "turtles."

"These guys are so cute, and that's what attracts us to them.
But they're also very sophisticated animals,
perfectly adapted to their environment."
—GREG WHITTAKER

PHOTOGRAPHY CREDITS